FUNNY

QUOTES

―――――~―――――

QUOTES TO TICKLE YOUR FUNNY BONE & BRIGHTEN YOUR DAY

SUSHEEL LADWA

Author of *10,001 Quotes & Sayings*

ISBN: 1503399311
ISBN-13: 978-1503399310

Mamata and Vishwanath Ladwa

My Mother and Father

"All I Am, I Owe To You"

ACKNOWLEDGMENTS

Writing a book starts as a hobby, becomes a passion, and rules your dreams until it becomes a reality. I gave it time because it is my passion. I want to acknowledge the people that gave their time and support to help realize my passion.

I wanted to thank my wife, Preetha, for her patience, love and support through the blur of day and night with a month old baby. This book would not have been possible without her. Every time there is a knock on my office door, there enters a big beautiful smile that makes it all worth it – Ruhi, my daughter, my friend, my little philosopher and guide. The new bundle of joy of the family – Syon, he is a month old but has shown who the boss is.

My brother, Sunil, my sister-in-law, Sumitra, and kids, Shreya, Kushi, and Arya, for their love and faith in me.

Last but not the least, my editor Jesse Kimmel-Freeman, for all the cattle she chased while editing my book – Thank you!

All men are equal before fish. - Herbert Hoover

Behind every great man is a woman rolling her eyes.
- Jim Carrey

Don't have sex man. It leads to kissing and pretty
soon you have to start talking to them. - Steve
Martin

Don't marry a man to reform him - that's what
reform schools are for. - Mae West

Everything is funny, as long as it's happening to somebody else.

Get your facts first, then you can distort them as you please. - Mark Twain

---

Have you ever noticed that anybody driving slower than you is an idiot, and anyone going faster than you is a maniac? - George Carlin

Housework can't kill you, but why take a chance? - Phyllis Diller

I buy expensive suits. They just look cheap on me. - Warren Buffett

I haven't spoken to my wife in years. I didn't want to interrupt her. - Rodney Dangerfield

I never forget a face, but in your case I'll be glad to make an exception. - Groucho Marx

If two wrongs don't make a right, try three. - Laurence Peter

Marriage is a wonderful institution, but who would want to live in an institution? - H. L. Mencken

Not only is there no God, but try finding a plumber on Sunday. - Woody Allen

So, where's the Cannes Film Festival being held this year? - Christina Aguilera

To err is human - but it feels divine. - Mae West

What is a wedding? Webster's dictionary defines a wedding as 'the process of removing weeds from one's garden.' - Homer Simpson

Who picks your clothes- Stevie Wonder? - Don Rickles

You're only as good as your last haircut. - Fran Lebowitz

A child of five would understand this. Send someone to fetch a child of five. - Groucho Marx

A committee is a group that keeps minutes and loses hours. - Milton Berle

A day without sunshine is like, you know, night. - Steve Martin

A government that robs Peter to pay Paul can always depend on the support of Paul. - George Bernard Shaw

A guy could have one major limb lying on the ground a full ten feet from the rest of his body, and he'd claim it was 'just a sprain'. - Dave Barry

---

A James Cagney love scene is one where he lets the other guy live. - Bob Hope

---

A lot of baby boomers are baby bongers. - Kevin Nealon

A man has one hundred dollars and you leave him with two dollars, that's subtraction. - Mae West

---

A man in love is incomplete until he has married. Then he's finished. - Zsa Zsa Gabor

A man's got to take a lot of punishment to write a really funny book. - Ernest Hemingway

A nickel ain't worth a dime anymore. - Yogi Berra

A pessimist is a person who has had to listen to too many optimists. - Don Marquis

A stockbroker urged me to buy a stock that would triple its value every year. I told him, 'At my age, I don't even buy green bananas.' - Claude Pepper

A successful man is one who makes more money than his wife can spend. A successful woman is one who can find such a man. - Lana Turner

A sure cure for seasickness is to sit under a tree. - Spike Milligan

A two-year-old is kind of like having a blender, but you don't have a top for it. -Jerry Seinfield

A vegetarian is a person who won't eat anything that have children. - David Brenner

A woman's mind is cleaner than a man's: she changes it more often. - Oliver Herford

A word to the wise ain't necessary - it's the stupid ones that need the advice. - Bill Cosby

Actually being funny is mostly telling the truth about things. - Bernard Sahlins

Admit it, sport-utility-vehicle owners! It's shaped a little differently, but it's a station wagon! And you do not drive it across rivers! You drive it across the Wal-Mart parking lot! - Dave Barry

Age is something that doesn't matter, unless you are cheese. - Luis Bunuel

Ah, yes, divorce ... from the Latin word meaning to rip out a man's genitals through his wallet. - Robin Williams

All generalizations are false, including this one. - Mark Twain

All I've ever wanted was an honest week's pay for

an honest day's work. - Steve Martin

All my children inherited perfect pitch. - Chevy Chase

All of life's riddles are answered in the movies. - Steve Martin

All right everyone, line up alphabetically according to your height. - Casey Stengel

All the candy corn that was ever made was made in 1911. - Lewis Black

Always end the name of your child with a vowel, so that when you yell the name will carry. - Bill Cosby

Always remember that you are absolutely unique. Just like everyone else. - Margaret Mead

An optimist is a fellow who believes a housefly is looking for a way to get out. - George Jean Nathan

Any girl can be glamorous. All you have to do is stand still and look stupid. - Hedy Lamarr

Any kid will run any errand for you, if you ask at bedtime. - Red Skelton

Anyone can get old, all you have to do is live long enough. - Groucho Marx

Anyone who says he can see through a women is
missing a lot. - Groucho Marx

As a child my family's menu consisted of two
choices: take it or leave it. - Buddy Hackett

As a child, I was more afraid of tetanus shots than,
for example, Dracula. - Dave Barry

As a matter of principle, I never attend the first annual anything. - George Carlin

As a woman, I find it very embarrassing to be in a meeting and realize I'm the only one in the room with balls. - Rita Mae Brown

As far as I'm concerned, 'whom' is a word that was invented to make everyone sound like a butler. - Calvin Trillin

As I get older, I just prefer to knit. - Tracey Ullman

Back in the old days, most families were close-knit. Grown children and their parents continued to live together, under the same roof, sometimes in the same small, crowded room, year in and year out, until they died, frequently by strangulation. - Dave Barry

Basically my wife was immature. I'd be at home in my bath and she'd come in and sink my boats. - Woody Allen

Be obscure clearly. - E. B. White

Be thankful we're not getting all the government
we're not paying for. - Will Rogers

Because of the level of my chess game, I was able -
even against a weak opponent, such as my younger
brothers or the dog - to get myself checkmated in
under three minutes. I challenge any computer to do
it faster. - Dave Barry

Because of their size, parents may be difficult to discipline properly. - P. J. O'Rourke

---

Before I refuse to take your questions, I have an opening statement. - Ronald Reagan

---

Behind every successful man is a woman, behind her is his wife. - Groucho Marx

---

Best way to get rid of kitchen odors: Eat out. - Phyllis Diller

Big business never pays a nickel in taxes, according to Ralph Nader, who represents a big consumer organization that never pays a nickel in taxes. - Dave Barry

Boy, those French, they have a different word for everything! - Steve Martin

Brought up to respect the conventions, love had to end in marriage. I'm afraid it did. - Bette Davis

Buying the right computer and getting it to work properly is no more complicated than building a nuclear reactor from wristwatch parts in a darkened room using only your teeth. - Dave Barry

By all means let's be open-minded, but not so open-minded that our brains drop out. - Richard Dawkins

California is a fine place to live- if you happen to be an orange. - Fred Allen

---

Camping is nature's way of promoting the motel business. - Dave Barry

---

Carpe per diem - seize the check. - Robin Williams

Chaos in the midst of chaos isn't funny, but chaos in the midst of order is. - Steve Martin

---

Childbirth, as a strictly physical phenomenon, is comparable to driving a United Parcel truck through an inner tube. - Dave Barry

Children are smarter than any of us. Know how I know that? I don't know one child with a full time job and children. - Bill Hicks

Christopher Columbus, as everyone knows, is honored by posterity because he was the last to discover America. - James Joyce

Classical music gradually lost popularity because it is too complicated: you need twenty-five or thirty skilled musicians just to hum it properly. So people began to develop regular music. - Dave Barry

Cleanliness becomes more important when godliness is unlikely. - P. J. O'Rourke

Cocaine is God's way of telling someone that they're too rich. - Robin Williams

Comedy is simply a funny way of being serious. -
Peter Ustinov

Comedy is the art of making people laugh without
making them puke. - Steve Martin

Communism is like one big phone company. -
Lenny Bruce

Congress, after years of stalling, finally got around
to clearing the way for informal discussions that

might lead to possible formal talks that could potentially produce some kind of tentative agreements. - Dave Barry

Cure for an obsession: get another one. - Mason Cooley

Defy your own group. Rebel against yourself. - Cathy Guisewite

Design is a funny word. Some people think design

means how it looks. But of course, if you dig deeper, it's really how it works. - Steve Jobs

---

Do not let a flattering woman coax and wheedle you and deceive you; she is after your barn. – Hesiod

---

Do not worry about avoiding temptation. As you grow older it will avoid you. - Joey Adams

---

Don't forget Mother's Day. Or as they call it in Beverly Hills, Dad's Third Wife Day. - Jay Leno

Don't knock masturbation; it's sex with someone I love. - Woody Allen

Don't you wish you had a job like mine? All you have to do is think up a certain number of words! Plus, you can repeat words! And they don't even have to be true! - Dave Barry

Eighty percent of success is showing up. - Woody Allen

Electricity is really just organized lightning. - George Carlin

English? Who needs that? I'm never going to England. - Homer Simpson

Every cloud has its silver lining but it is sometimes a little difficult to get it to the mint. - Don Marquis

Every man has his follies- and often they are the most interesting thing he has got. - Josh Billings

Every man's dream is to be able to sink into the arms of a woman without also falling into her hands. - Jerry Lewis

Every time I see an adult on a bicycle, I no longer despair for the future of the human race. - H. G. Wells

Everybody talks about the weather, but nobody does anything about it. - Charles Dudley Warner

Everything in life is somewhere else, and you get there in a car. - E. B. White

Everything that used to be a sin is now a disease. - Bill Maher

Experience is what you have after you've forgotten her name. - Milton Berle

Fashions have done more harm than revolutions. - Victor Hugo

Fatherhood is pretending the present you love most is soap on-a-rope. - Bill Cosby

Fighting for peace is like screwing for virginity. - George Carlin

First the doctor told me the good news: I was going to have a disease named after me. - Steve Martin

———————～————

Flattery is like cologne water, to be smelt, not swallowed. - Josh Billings

———————～————

Food is an important part of a balanced diet. - Fran Lebowitz

———————～————

Food, love, career, and mothers, the four major guilt groups. - Cathy Guisewite

For two people in a marriage to live together day after day is unquestionably the one miracle the Vatican has overlooked. - Bill Cosby

Frawing on my fine command of the English language, I said nothing. - Robert Benchley

Frisbeetarianism is the belief that when you die, your soul goes up on the roof and gets stuck. - George Carlin

From the moment I picked your book up until I laid it down I was convulsed with laughter. Someday I intend reading it. - Groucho Marx

From there to here, and here to there, funny things are everywhere. - Theodore Seuss

Getting divorced just because you don't love a man is almost as silly as getting married just because you do. - Zsa Zsa Gabor

Give a man a free hand and he'll run it all over you.
- Mae West

Go to Heaven for the climate, Hell for the company.
- Mark Twain

God did not intend religion to be an exercise club. -
Naguib Mahfouz

Good sex is like good Bridge: if you don't have a good partner, you'd better have a good hand. - Mae West

Guilt: the gift that keeps on giving. - Erma Bombeck

Happiness is having a large loving, caring, close-knit family in another city. - George Burns

Have enough sense to know, ahead of time, when your skills will not extend to wallpapering. -

Marilyn von Savant

Have you noticed that whatever sport you're trying to learn, some earnest person is always telling you to keep your knees bent? - Dave Barry

He looks as though he's been weaned on a pickle. - Alice Roosevelt Longworth

Honesty may be the best policy, but it's important to remember that apparently, by elimination, dishonesty is the second-best policy. - George Carlin

Hosting the Oscars is like making love to a beautiful woman - it's something I only get to do when Billy Crystal's out of town. - Steve Martin

How long was I in the army? Five foot eleven. - Spike Milligan

How many people here have telekinetic powers? Raise my hand. - Emo Philips

I always just wanted to be funny. I never really planned to be scary. - R. L. Stine

I always wanted to be somebody, but now I realize I should have been more specific. - Lily Tomlin

I am certain there is too much certainty in the world. - Michael Crichton

I am not a member of any organized political party.
I am a Democrat. - Will Rogers

I argue very well. Ask any of my remaining friends.
I can win an argument on any topic, against any
opponent. People know this, and steer clear of me at
parties. Often, as a sign of their great respect, they
don't even invite me. - Dave Barry

I basically started performing for my mother, going,
'Love me!' What drives you to perform is the need
for that primal connection. When I was little, my
mother was funny with me, and I started to be
charming and funny for her, and I learned that
being entertaining you make a connection with
another person. - Robin Williams

I believe that if life gives you lemons, you should make lemonade … and try to find somebody whose life has given them vodka, and have a party. - Ron White

I believe that sex is a beautiful thing between two people. Between five, it's fantastic. - Woody Allen

I believe that sex is one of the most beautiful, natural, wholesome things that money can buy. - Steve Martin

I bought some batteries, but they weren't included. - Steven Wright

I can speak Esperanto like a native. - Spike Milligan

I cannot sing, dance or act; what else would I be but a talk show host. - David Letterman

I consider that a man's brain originally is like a little empty attic, and you have to stock it with such furniture as you choose. - Arthur Conan Doyle

I cook with wine, sometimes I even add it to the food. - W. C. Fields

I could not handle being a woman, I would stay home all day and play with my breasts. - Steve Martin

I did not have three thousand pairs of shoes, I had one thousand and sixty. - Imelda Marcos

I distrust camels, and anyone else who can go a week without a drink. - Joe E. Lewis

I don't believe in after life, although I am bringing a change of underwear. - Woody Allen

I don't deserve this award, but I have arthritis and I don't deserve that either. - Jack Benny

I don't get no respect! - Rodney Dangerfield

I don't need you to remind me of my age. I have a bladder to do that for me. - Stephen Fry

I don't want to achieve immortality through my work; I want to achieve immortality through not dying. - Woody Allen

I don't have a bank account because I don't know my mother's maiden name. - Paula Poundstone

I don't think anyone should write their autobiography until after they're dead. - Samuel Goldwyn

I drank some boiling water because I wanted to whistle. - Mitch Hedberg

I failed to make the chess team because of my

height. - Woody Allen

I feel sorry for short people, you know. When it rains, they're the last to know. - Rodney Dangerfield

I found there was only one way to look thin: hang out with fat people. - Rodney Dangerfield

I generally avoid temptation unless I can't resist it. - Mae West

I got attention by being funny at school, pretending to be retarded, and jumping around with a deformed hard. - Leonardo DiCaprio

I grew up in Europe, where the history comes from. - Eddie Izzard

I guess when you turn off the main road, you have to be prepared to see some funny houses. - Stephen King

I hate housework! You make the beds, you do the dishes and six months later you have to start all over again. - Joan Rivers

I hate rap music, which to me sounds like a bunch of angry men shouting, possibly because the person who was supposed to provide them with a melody never showed up. - Dave Barry

I have a new philosophy. I'm only going to dread one day at a time. - Charles Schulz

I have a very low level of recognition, which is fine by me. - Dylan Moran

I have an intense desire to return to the womb. Anybody's. - Woody Allen

I have never been hurt by what I have not said. - Calvin Coolidge

I have six locks on my door all in a row. When I go out, I lock every other one. I figure no matter how long somebody stands there picking the locks, they are always locking three. - Elayne Boosler

I have tried to know absolutely nothing about a great many things, and I have succeeded fairly well. - Robert Benchley

I have yet to hear a man ask for advice on how to combine marriage and a career. - Gloria Steinem

I knew I was an unwanted baby when I saw that my bath toys were a toaster and a radio. - Joan Rivers

I know nothing about sex because I was always married. - Zsa Zsa Gabor

I like long walks, especially when they are taken by people who annoy me. - Fred Allen

I like marriage. The idea. - Toni Morrison

I like to say that I'm bisexual ... when I want sex, I buy it. - Boy George

I liked children- fried. - W. C. Fields

I looked up my family tree and found out I was the sap. - Rodney Dangerfield

I love deadlines. I like the whooshing sound they make as they fly by. -Douglas Adams

I love Mickey Mouse more than any woman I have ever known. - Walt Disney

I love Thanksgiving. It's the only time in Los Angeles that you see natural breasts. - Arnold Schwarzenegger

I love to go to Washington- if only to be near my

money. - Bob Hope

I may be a living legend, but that sure don't help when I've got to change a flat tire. - Roy Orbison

I never drink water because of the disgusting things that fish do in it. - W. C. Fields

I never expected to see the day when girls would get sunburned in the places they now do. - Will Rogers

I never hated a man enough to give him diamonds
back. - Zsa Zsa Gabor

I never said most of the things I said. - Yogi Berra

I no doubt deserved my enemies, but I don't believe
I deserved my friends. - Walt Whitman

I quite therapy because my analyst was trying to help me behind my back. - Richard Lewis

I rant, therefore I am. - Dennis Miller

I realise that I'm making gender-based generalizations here, but my feeling is that if God did not want us to make gender-based generalizations, she would not have given us genders. - Dave Barry

I recently had my annual physical examination, which I get once every seven years, and when the nurse weighed me, I was shocked to discover how much stronger the Earth's gravitational pull has become since 1990. - Dave Barry

I recorded my hair this morning, tonight I'm watching the highlights. - Jay London

I sang in the choir for years, even though my family, belonged to another church. - Paul Lynde

I saw a woman wearing a sweatshirt with Guess on it. I said, Thyroid problem? - Arnold Schwarzenegger

I saw this in a movie about a bus that had to SPEED around a city, keeping its SPEED over fifty, and if its SPEED dropped, it would explode! I think it was called, 'The Bus That Couldn't Slow Down.' - Homer Simpson

I spent a year in that town, one Sunday. - George Burns

I think it's the duty of the comedian to find out where the line is drawn and cross it deliberately. - George Carlin

I think serial monogamy says it all. - Tracey Ullman

I think they should have a Barbie with a buzz cut. - Ellen DeGeneres

I told my psychiatrist that everyone hates me. He said I was being ridiculous - everyone hasn't met me

yet. - Rodney Dangerfield

I used to be Snow White, but I drifted. - Mae West

I used to jog but the ice cubes kept falling out of my glass. - David Lee Roth

I used to sell furniture for a living. The trouble was, it was my own. - Les Dawson

I wanna make a jigsaw puzzle that's 40,000 pieces. And when you finish it, it says 'go outside.' - Demetri Martin

I was a vegetarian until I started leaning toward the sunlight. - Rita Rudner

I was born in very sorry circumstances. Both of my parents were very sorry. - Norman Wisdom

I was eating in a Chinese restaurant downtown. There was a dish called Mother and Child Reunion. It's chicken and eggs. And I said, I gotta use that one. - Paul Simon

I was sleeping the other night, alone, thanks to the exterminator. - Emo Philips

I was so naïve as a kid I used to sneak behind the barn and do nothing. - Johnny Carson

I was the kid next door's imaginary friend. - Emo
Philips

I was thrown out of college for cheating on the
metaphysics exam: I looked into the soul of another
boy. - Woody Allen

I wear a necklace, cause I wanna know when I'm
upside down. - Mitch Hedberg

I went to a fight last night and a hockey game broke out. - Rodney Dangerfield

I went window shopping today! I bought four windows. - Tommy Cooper

I wish I had the nerve not to tip. - Paul Lynde

I would never die for my beliefs because I might be wrong. - Bertrand Russell

I would not join any club that would have someone like me for a member. - Groucho Marx

I would not know how I am supposed to feel about many stories if not for the fact that the TV news personalities make sad faces for sad stories and happy faces for happy stories. - Dave Barry

I would talk in iambic pentameter if it were easier. - Howard Nemerov

I'd luv to kiss ya, but I just washed my hair. - Bette Davis

I'd never been in play long enough for the flowers to die in the dressing room. - Mercedes McCambridge

I'll always perform, because show business is in my blood. Or maybe it's in my feet. Wherever it is, I don't think I'll ever stop. - Robin Williams

I'm a great housekeeper: I get divorced, I keep the house. - Zsa Zsa Gabor

I'm a misplaced American, but don't know where I was misplaced. - Ruby Wax

I'm an idealist. I don't know where I'm going, but I'm on my way. - Carl Sandburg

I'm astounded by people who want to 'know' the universe when it's hard enough to find your way around Chinatown. -Woody Allen

I'm at an age where I think more about food than sex. Last week I put a mirror over my dining room table. - Rodney Dangerfield

I'm completely in favor of the separation of Church and State. My idea is that these two institutions screw us up enough on their own, so both of them together is certain death. - George Carlin

I'm for whatever gets you through the night. - Frank Sinatra

I'm going to marry a Jewish woman because I like the idea of getting up on Sunday morning and going to the deli. - Michael J. Fox

I'm kidding about having only a few dollars. I might have a few dollars more. - James Brown

I'm like that guy who single-handedly built the rocket & flew to the moon! What was his name? Apollo Creed? - Homer Simpson

I'm not afraid of death, I just don't want to be there when it happens. - Woody Allen

I'm not concerned about all hell breaking loose, but that a PART of hell will break loose ... it'll be much harder to detect. - George Carlin

I'm not funny. What I am is brave. - Lucille Ball

I'm not normally a religious man, but if you're up there, save me, Superman! - Homer Simpson

I'm not popular enough to be different. - Homer Simpson

I'm not upset about my divorce. I'm only upset I'm not a widow. - Roseanne Barr

---

I'm sorry, if you were right, I'd agree with you. - Robin Williams

---

I'm spending a year dead for tax reasons. - Douglas Adams

I'm thankful for the three ounce Ziploc bag, so that I have somewhere to put my savings. - Paula

Poundstone

I'm the only man in the world with a marriage license made out to whom it may concern. - Mickey Rooney

I'm undaunted in my quest to amuse myself by constantly changing my hair. - Hillary Clinton

I'm very proud of my gold pocket watch. My grandfather, on his deathbed, sold me this watch. -

Woody Allen

I'm writing a book. I've got the page numbers done.
- Steven Wright

I've always wanted to go to Switzerland to see what
the army does with those wee red knives. - Billy
Connolly

I've got more trophies than Wayne Gretzky & The
Pope combined! - Homer Simpson

I've had a wonderful time, but this wasn't it. -
Groucho Marx

I've never been married, but I tell people I'm
divorced so they won't think something is wrong
with me. - Elayne Boosler

If a woman has to choose between catching a fly ball
and saving an infant's life, she will choose to save
the infant's life without even considering if there are
men on base. - Dave Barry

If at first you don't succeed, blame your parents. - Marcelene Cox

If at first you don't succeed… so much for skydiving. - Henny Youngman

If at first you don't succeed, find out if the loser gets anything. - William Lyon Phelps

If God didn't want us to eat animals, why did he make them out of meat? - Homer Simpson

If God had wanted us to be concerned for the plight of the toads, he would have made them cute and furry. - Dave Barry

If God had wanted us to spend our time fretting about the problems of home ownership, He would never have invented beer. - Dave Barry

If God wanted us to bend over he'd put diamonds on the floor. - Joan Rivers

If God wanted us to fly, He would have given us tickets. - Mel Brooks

If he's so smart, how come he's dead? - Homer Simpson

If I had to live my life again, I'd make the same mistakes, only sooner. - Tallulah Bankhead

If I knew for a certainty that a man was coming to my house with a conscious design of doing my good, I should run for my life. - Henry David Thoreau

If I want to knock a story off the front page, I just change my hairstyle. - Hillary Clinton

If it weren't for Phil T. Farnsworth, inventor of television, we'd still be eating frozen radio dinners. - Johnny Carson

If it's the Psychic Network why do they need a phone number? - Robin Williams

If love is the answer, could you please rephrase the question? - Lily Tomlin

If men knew how women pass the time when they are alone, they'd never marry. - O. Henry

If only God would give me some clear sign! Like making a large deposit in my name in a Swiss bank. - Woody Allen

If the new American father feels bewildered and even defeated, let him take comfort from the fact that whatever he does in any fathering situation has a fifty percent chance of being right. - Bill Cosby

If truth is beauty, how come no one has their hair done in the library? - Lily Tomlin

If you are not failing every now and again, it's a sign you're playing it safe. - Woody Allen

If you can't get rid of the skeleton in your closet, you'd best teach it to dance. - George Bernard Shaw

If you can't tell a spoon from a ladle, then you're fat! - Demetri Martin

If you could kick the person in the pants responsible for most of your trouble, you wouldn't sit for a

month. - Theodore Roosevelt

If you had to identify, in one word, the reason why the human race has not achieved, and never will achieve its full potential, that word would be meetings. - Dave Barry

If you have a secret, people will sit a little bit closer. - Rod Corddry

If you live to be one hundred, you've got it made.

Very few people die past that age. - George Burns

If you surveyed a hundred typical middle-aged Americans, I bet you'd find that only two of them could tell you their blood types, but every last one of them would know the theme song from The Beverly Hillbillies. - Dave Barry

If you want a guarantee, buy a toaster. - Clint Eastwood

If you want to be thought a liar, always tell the truth. - Logan Pearsall Smith

If you were to open up a baby's head -- and I am not for a moment suggesting that you should -- you would find nothing but an enormous drool gland. - Dave Barry

If you're going to do something tonight that you'll be sorry for tomorrow morning, sleep late. - Henny Youngman

In comic strips, the person on the left always speaks first. - George Carlin

In fact, just about all the major natural attractions you find in the West -- the Grand Canyon, the Badlands, the Goodlands, the Mediocrelands, the Rocky Mountains and Robert Redford -- were caused by erosion. - Dave Barry

It all started when my dog began getting free roll over minutes. - Jay London

It always rains on tents. Rainstorms will travel thousands of miles, against prevailing winds for the opportunity to rain on a tent. - Dave Barry

It is a good idea to "shop around" before you settle on a doctor. Ask about the condition of his Mercedes. Ask about the competence of his mechanic. Don't be shy! After all, you're paying for it. - Dave Barry

It is a scientific fact that your body will not absorb cholesterol if you take it from another person's plate. - Dave Barry

It is easy for me to love myself, but for ladies to do it is another question altogether. - Johnny Vegas

---

It is even harder for the average ape to believe that he has descended from man. - H. L. Mencken

---

It is impossible to experience one's death objectively and still carry a tune. - Woody Allen

---

It is impossible to travel faster than the speed of light, and certainly not desirable, as one's hat keeps

blowing off. - Woody Allen

It must be so humiliating to have such a public break-up. - Ellen DeGeneres to Justin Timberlake

It seemed the world was divided into good and bad people. The good ones slept better, while the bad ones seemed to enjoy the waking hours much more. - Woody Allen

It takes considerable knowledge just to realize the

extent of your own ignorance. - Thomas Sowell

It's always funny until someone gets hurt. Then it's just hilarious. - Bill Hicks

It's amazing that the amount of news that happens in the world every day always just exactly fits in the newspaper. - Jerry Seinfield

It's simple, if it jiggles, it's fat. - Arnold Schwarzenegger

Karate is a form of marital arts in which people who have had years and years of training can, using only their hands and feet, make some of the worst movies in the history of the world. - Dave Barry

Keep your sense of humor, my friend; if you don't have a sense of humor it just isn't funny anymore. - Wavy Gravy

———

Kids like my act because I'm wearing nose glasses. Adults like my act because there's a guy who thinks putting on nose glasses is funny. - Steve Martin

Kids, just because I don't care doesn't mean I'm not listening. - Homer Simpson

Last night I discovered a new form of oral contraceptive. I asked a girl to go to bed with me and she said no. - Woody Allen

Laugh and the world laughs with you, snore and you sleep alone. - Anthony Burgress

Let us celebrate our agreement with the adding of chocolate to milk. - Homer Simpson

Let us now set forth one of the fundamental truths about marriage: the wife is in charge. - Bill Cosby

Life is anything that dies when you stomp on it. - Dave Barry

Life is hard. After all, it kills you. - Katherine Hepburn

Life would be tragic if it weren't funny. -Stephen Hawking

Like everyone else who makes the mistake of getting older, I begin each day with coffee and obituaries. - Bill Cosby

Like many members of the uncultured, Cheez-It

consuming public, I am not good at grasping modern art. - Dave Barry

Look closely at Central America, and try to imagine what would happen if this vital region were to fall into Communist hands. What would happen is a lot of Communists would be stung repeatedly by vicious tropical insects the size of mature hamsters. - Dave Barry

Look, all I'm saying is, if these big stars didn't want people going through their garbage and saying they're gay, then they shouldn't have tried to express themselves creatively. - Homer Simpson

Love is the answer, but while you are waiting for the answer, sex raises some pretty good questions. - Woody Allen

Magnetism is one of the Six Fundamental Forces of the Universe, with the other five being Gravity, Duct Tape, Whining, Remote Control, and The Force That Pulls Dogs Toward The Groins Of Strangers. - Dave Barry

Magnetism, as you recall from physics class, is a powerful force that causes certain items to be attracted to refrigerators. - Dave Barry

Mail your packages early so the post office can lose them in time for Christmas. - Johnny Carson

Man cannot live by bread alone; he must have peanut butter. - James Garfield

Me carrying a briefcase is like a hotdog wearing earrings. - Sparky Anderson

Meetings are an addictive, highly self-indulgent activity that corporations and other large organizations habitually engage in only because they cannot actually masturbate. - Dave Barry

MEGAHERTZ: This is a really, really big hertz. - Dave Barry

Men are liars. We'll lie about lying if we have to. I'm an algebra liar. I figure two good lies make a positive. - Tim Allen

Men are only as loyal as their options. - Bill Maher

Miami Beach is where neon goes to die. - Lenny Bruce

Moderation is a virtue only in those who are thought to have an alternative. - Henry Kissinger

Money doesn't make you happy. I now have $50 million, but I was just as happy when I had $48 million. - Arnold Schwarzenegger

Money is better than poverty, if only for financial reasons. - Woody Allen

More than any time in history mankind faces a crossroads. One path leads to despair and utter hopelessness, the other to total extinction. Let us pray that we have the wisdom to choose correctly. - Woody Allen

Most comedy is based on getting a laugh at somebody else's expense. And I find that that's just a form of bullying in a major way. So I want to be an example that you can be funny and be kind, and

make people laugh without hurting somebody else's feelings. - Ellen DeGeneres

My definition of an intellectual is someone who can listen to the William Tell Overture without thinking of the Lone Ranger. - Billy Connolly

My fake plants died because I did not pretend to water them. - Mitch Hedberg

My father would take me to the playground, and

put me on mood swings. - Jay London

My grandmother started walking five miles a day when she was sixty. She's ninety-five now, and we don't know where the hell she is. - Ellen DeGeneres

My life needs editing. - Mort Sahl

My mother used to say to me: "Son, it's better to be rich and healthy than poor and sick." I think that still makes a heck of a lot of sense, even in these

troubles times. - Dave Barry

My mother was against me being an actress- until I introduced her to Frank Sinatra. - Angie Dickinson

My one regret in life is that I am not someone else. - Woody Allen

My theory is that all Scottish cuisine is based on a dare. - Mike Meyers

My therapist told me the way to achieve true inner peace is to finish what I start. So far today, I have finished 2 bags of M&M's and a chocolate cake. I feel better already. - Dave Barry

My uncle Sammy was an angry man. He had printed on his tombstone: What are you looking at?
- Margaret Smith

My wife has a slight impediment in her speech. Every now and then she stops to breathe. - Jimmy Durante

Never fight an inanimate object. - P. J. O'Rourke

Never have more children than you have car windows. - Erma Bombeck

Never put a sock in a toaster. - Eddie Izzard

No, no, no, Lisa. If adults don't like their jobs, they don't go on strike. They just go in every day and do it really half-assed. - Homer Simpson

Nobody cares if you can't dance well. Just get up and dance. - Dave Barry

Nobody ever went broke underestimating the taste of the American public. - H. L. Mencken

Not all chemicals are bad. Without chemicals such

as hydrogen and oxygen, for example, there would be no way to make water, a vital ingredient in beer. - Dave Barry

O Lord, help me to be pure, but not yet. - Saint Augustine

Old people don't need companionship. They need to be isolated and studied so it can be determined what nutrients they have that might be extracted for our personal use. - Homer Simpson

Older people shouldn't eat health food, they need all the preservatives they can get. - Robert Orben

On the plus side, death is one of the few things that can be done just as easily lying down. - Woody Allen

Once again, we come to the Holiday Season, a deeply religious time that each of us observes, in his own way, by going to the mall of his choice. - Dave Barry

One man is as good as another until he has written a book. - Benjamin Jowett

---

One man's folly is another man's wife. -Helen Rowland

One picture is worth 1,000 denials. - Ronald Reagan

Only one man in a thousand is a leader of men. The other 999 follow women. - Groucho Marx

Only the mediocre are always at their best. - Jean
Giraudoux

Originality is the fine art of remembering what you
hear but forgetting where you heard it. - Laurence
Peter

Our national flower is the concrete cloverleaf. -
Lewis Mumford

Outside of a dog, a book is a man's best friend.
Inside of a dog, it is too dark to read. - Groucho
Marx

Parents are not interested in justice, they're
interested in peace and quiet. - Bill Cosby

Parents are the last people on earth who ought to
have children. - Samuel Butler

Parrots make great pets. They have more personality than goldfish. - Chevy Chase

Part of my act is meant to shake you up. It looks like I'm being funny, but I'm reminding you of other things. Life is tough, darling. Life is hard. And we better laugh at everything; otherwise, we're going down the tube. - Joan Rivers

People always ask me, 'Were you funny as a child?' Well, no, I was an accountant. -Ellen DeGeneres

People say that life is the thing, but I prefer reading.
-Logan Pearsall Smith

People who think they know everything are a great
annoyance to those of us that do. - Isaac Asimov

People who want to share their religious views with
you almost never want you to share yours with
them. - Dave Barry

Politics is the art of looking for trouble, finding it everywhere, diagnosing it incorrectly, and applying the wrong remedies. - Groucho Marx

---

Procrastination is the art of keeping up with yesterday. - Don Marquis

---

Progress was all right. Only it went on too long. - James Thurber

Quote me as saying I was mis-quoted. - Groucho Marx

Reality continues to ruin my life. - Bill Watterson

Remember, if you smoke after sex you're doing it too fast. - Woody Allen

Roses are red, violets are blue, I'm schizophrenic,
and so am I. - Oscar Levant

Scientists tell us that the fastest animal on earth,
with a top speed of 120 ft/sec, is a cow that has been
dropped out of a helicopter. - Dave Barry

Sex alleviates tension. Love causes it. - Woody Allen

Sex is only dirty if it's done right. - Woody Allen

Sex without love is a meaningless experience, but as far as meaningless experiences go, it's pretty damn good. - Woody Allen

She was a handsome woman of forty-five and would remain so for many years. - J. B. Priestley

Skiing combines outdoor fun with knocking down trees with your face. - Dave Barry

Smoking kills. If you're killed, you've lost a very important part of your life. - Brooke Shields

Snowboarding is an activity that is very popular with people who do not feel that regular skiing is lethal enough. - Dave Barry

Society is like a stew. If you don't stir it up every once in a while then a layer of scum floats to the top. - Edward Abbey

Some national parks have long waiting lists for camping reservations. When you have to wait a year to sleep next to a tree, something is wrong. - George Carlin

Someone told me that when they go to Vermont, they feel like they're home. I'm that way at Saks. - Caroline Rhea

Stand-up comedy is transient. History shows that you can stand up for so long; after that, you're asked to sit down. - Steve Martin

Talking about golf is always boring. (Playing golf can be interesting, but not the part where you try to hit the little ball; only the part where you drive the cart.) - Dave Barry

Talking about music is like dancing about architecture. - Steve Martin

Television has brought back murder into the home - where it belongs. - Alfred Hitchcock

Television is where you watch people in your living room that you would not want near your house. - Groucho Marx

That's my only goal. Surround myself with funny people, and make sure everyone has a good time and works hard. - Joe Rogan

The ACLU is always yakking about the Constitution, and most of us are getting mighty tired of it. I mean, if the Constitution is so great, how come it was amended so many times? Huh? - Dave Barry

The best ideas come as jokes. Make your thinking as funny as possible. - David Ogilvy

The best measure of a man's honesty isn't his income tax return. It's the zero adjust on his bathroom scale. - Arthur C. Clarke

The cool thing about being famous is traveling. I have always wanted to travel across seas, like to Canada and stuff. - Britney Spears

The day I made that statement about the inventing the internet, I was tired because I'd been up all night inventing the Camcorder. - Al Gore

The Democrats seem to be basically nicer people, but they have demonstrated time and again that they have the management skills of celery. - Dave Barry

The difference between sex and death is that with death you can do it alone and no one is going to make fun of you. - Woody Allen

The first time I sang in the church choir; two
hundred people changed their religion. - Fred Allen

The four building blocks of the universe are fire,
water, gravel and vinyl. - Dave Barry

The funny thing is, I'm so used to not caring what
anyone says, good or bad, that unfortunately even
when people say good things … I wish it made me
feel good, but it doesn't. - Rob Zombie

The good thing about being bisexual is that it doubles your chance of a date on a Saturday night. - Woody Allen

The greatest thing you can do is surprise yourself. - Steve Martin

The important thing, I think, is not to be bitter ... if it turns about that there is a God, I don't think that he is evil. I think that the worst thing you could say is that he is, basically, an under-achiever. - Woody Allen

The information encoded in your DNA determines your unique biological characteristics, such as sex, eye color, age and Social Security number. - Dave Barry

The Internet is a giant international network of intelligent, informed computer enthusiasts, by which I mean, "people without lives." We don't care. We have each other ... - Dave Barry

The Internet: Transforming Society and Shaping the Future Through Chat. - Dave Barry

The IQ and the life expectancy of the average American recently passed each other going in the opposite direction. - George Carlin

The IRS! They're like the Mafia, they can take anything they want! - Jerry Seinfield

The last time I saw him he was walking down lover's land holding his own hand. - Fred Allen

The leading cause of death among fashion models is falling through street grates. - Dave Barry

The major parties could conduct live human sacrifices on their podiums during prime time, and I doubt that anybody would notice. - Dave Barry

The next time you have a thought ... let it go. - Ron White

The one thing that unites all human beings, regardless of age, gender, religion, economic status or ethnic background, is that, deep down inside, we ALL believe that we are above- average drivers. - Dave Barry

The one thing you shouldn't do is try to tell a cab driver how to get somewhere. - Jimmy Fallon

The only kind of seafood I trust is the fish stick, a totally featureless fish that doesn't have eyeballs or fins. - Dave Barry

The only monster here is the gambling monster that has enslaved your mother! I call him Gamblor, and it's time to snatch your mother from his neon claws!
- Homer Simpson

The only really good place to buy lumber is at a store where the lumber has already been cut and attached together in the form of furniture, finished, and put inside boxes. - Dave Barry

The only time I ever enjoyed ironing was the day I accidentally got gin in the steam iron. - Phyllis Diller

The reason there are two senators for each state is so that one can be the designated driver. - Jay Leno

The statistics on sanity are that one out of every four Americans are suffering from some form of mental illness. Think of your three best friends. If they're okay, then it's you. - Rita Mae Brown

The superfluous, a very necessary thing. – Voltaire

The trouble with having an open mind, of course, is that people will insist on coming along and trying to put things in it. - Terry Pratchett

The way taxes are, you might as well marry for love.
- Joe E. Lewis

The world is full of magical things patiently waiting for our wits to grow sharper. - Bertrand Russell

There are lots of people who mistake their imagination for their memory. - Josh Billings

There are no seeing eye cats, of course, because the sole function of cats, in the Great Chain of Life, is to cause harm to human beings. - Dave Barry

There are only three things women need in life: food, water, and compliments. - Chris Rock

There cannot be a crisis next week. My schedule is already full. - Henry Kissinger

There is no question that there is an unseen world. The problem is, how far is it from midtown and how late is it open? - Woody Allen

There is nothing funny about Halloween. This sarcastic festival reflects, rather, an infernal demand for revenger by children on the adult world. - Jean Baudrillard

There is one thing I would break up over, and that is if she caught me with another woman. I won't stand for that. - Steve Martin

There's a great power in words, if you don't hitch too many of them together. - Josh Billings

There's an old joke... two elderly women are at a Catskill mountain resort, and one of 'em says, "Boy, the food at this place is really terrible." The other one says, "Yeah, I know; and such small portions." Well, that's essentially how I feel about life - full of loneliness, and misery, and suffering, and unhappiness - and it's all over much too quickly. - Woody Allen

─────── ～ ───────

There's no present. There's only the immediate future and the recent past. - George Carlin

─────── ～ ───────

There's no such thing as soy milk. It's soy juice. - Lewis Black

─────── ～ ───────

There's nothing wrong with being shallow as long as you're insightful about it. - Dennis Miller

There's one thing about baldness, it's neat. - Don Herold

They say marriages are made in Heaven. But so is thunder and lightning. - Clint Eastwood

Thinking is one thing no one has ever been able to tax. - Charles Kettering

This suspense is terrible. I hope it will last. - Oscar Wilde

Those are my principles. If you don't like them I have others. - Groucho Marx

Thus the metric system did not really catch on in the States, unless you count the increasing popularity of the nine-millimeter bullet. - Dave Barry

To label me an intellectual is a misunderstanding of

what that is. - Dick Cavett

Too much agreement kills a chat. - Eldridge Cleaver

Too much of a good thing can be wonderful. - Mae West

Tragedy is when I cut my finger. Comedy is when you fall into an open sewer and die. - Mel Brooks

Trust is hard to come by. That's why my circle is small and tight. I'm kind of funny about making new friends. – Eminem

TV is chewing gum for the eyes. - Frank Lloyd Wright

Two wrongs don't make a right, but they make a good excuse. - Thomas Szasz

Until you walk a mile in another man's moccasins you can't imagine the smell. - Robert Byrne

We are all here on earth to help others; what on earth the others are here for I don't know. - W. H. Auden

We humans do not need to leave Earth to get to a hostile, deadly, alien environment; we already have Miami. - Dave Barry

We know that the nature of genius is to provide idiots with ideas twenty years later. - Louise Aragon

We need two kinds of acquaintances, one to complain to, while to the others we boast. - Logan Pearsall Smith

We'll love you just the way you are if you're perfect. - Alanis Morissette

We'll try to cooperate fully with the IRS, because, as citizens, we feel a strong patriotic duty not to go to jail. - Dave Barry

Weaseling out of things is important to learn. It's what separates us from the animals ... except the weasel. - Homer Simpson

Weather forecast for tonight: dark. - George Carlin

Well, if crime fighters fight crime and fire fighters fight fire, what do freedom fighters fight? They never mention that part to us, do they? - George Carlin

Well, if I called the wrong number, why did you answer the phone? - James Thurber

What contemptible scoundrel has stolen the cork to my lunch? - W. Clement Stone

What happens if a big asteroid hits Earth? Judging from realistic simulations involving a sledge hammer and a common laboratory frog, we can assume it will be pretty bad. - Dave Barry

What I just said is the fundamental, end-all, final, not-subject-to-opinion absolute truth, depending on where you're standing. - Steve Martin

What's another word for Thesaurus? - Steven Wright

When I eventually met Mr. Right I had no idea that his first name was Always. - Rita Rudner

When choosing between two evils, I always like to try the one I've never tried before. - Mae West

When I first heard that Marge was joining the police academy, I thought it would be fun and zany, like that movie Spaceballs. But instead it was dark and disturbing. Like that movie -- Police Academy. - Homer Simpson

When I go to a bar, I don't go looking for a girl who knows the capital of Maine. - David Brenner

When I was a boy the Dead Sea was only sick. - George Burns

When I was born I owed twelve dollars. - George S. Kaufman

When Jonathan Winters died, it was like, 'Oh, man!' I knew he was frail, but I always thought he was going to last longer. I knew as being really funny, but at the same time, he had a dark side. - Robin Williams

When we played softball, I'd steal second base, feel guilty and go back. - Woody Allen

When we talk to God, we're praying. When God talks to us, we're schizophrenic. - Jane Wagner

When you are courting a nice girl an hour seems like a second. When you sit on a red-hot cinder a second seems like an hour. That's relativity. - Albert Einstein

When you become senile, you won't know it. - Bill Cosby

When you get right down to it, the Safety Lecture is a silly idea. I mean, if the passengers really thought the plane was going to crash, they wouldn't get on it in the first place, let alone learn how to get an adequate oxygen supply on the way down. - Dave Barry

When you're eight years old nothing is your
business. - Lenny Bruce

When you're in love it's the most glorious two and a
half days of your life. - Richard Lewis

Whoever is my relative, I will not be nice to them. -
George Lopez

Why do they call it rush hour when nothing moves?
- Robin Williams

Why don't you get out of that wet coat and into a
dry martini? - Robert Benchley

Wine is constant proof that God loves us and loves
to see us happy. - Benjamin Franklin

Women don't want to hear what you think. Women
want to hear what they think in a deeper voice. - Bill

Cosby

Women should be obscene and not heard. - Groucho Marx

Working with Julie Andrews is like getting hit over the head with a valentine. - Christopher Plummer

You can lead a man to Congress, but you can't make him think. - Milton Berle

You can only be young once but you can be
immature forever. - Dave Barry

You can say any foolish thing to a dog, and the dog
will give you a look that says, "My God, you're
right! I never would've thought of that!" - Dave
Barry

You can't really be strong until you see a funny side
of things. - Ken Kesey

You know what your problem is? It's that you haven't seen enough movies - all of life's riddles are answered in the movies. - Steve Martin

You see much more of your children once they leave home. - Lucille Ball

You should do your own car repairs. It's an easy way to save money and possibly maim yourself for life. - Dave Barry

You're never too old to become younger. - Mae West

About the Author

 Growing up in a small town in India, Susheel heard a story. A child goes to a fair and sees a man selling balloons; he watches the red balloon fly away high into the sky. He asks the balloon vendor, "Will the green balloon fly into the sky as well?" The balloon man says, "Yes." Next the child asks, "How about the black balloon?" The balloon vendor replies, "It is not the color of the balloon, but what is in it that takes the balloon high into the sky."

Susheel has lived with a strong belief that "it is what you have in you that takes you the places you want to go, it does not matter where you come from, all that matters is where you are going."

Susheel has a passion for quotes, sayings, and studying interesting facts about history and their relevance in the modern world. In the past decade, he has consulted with fortune 500 clients advising them on business strategies.

Made in the USA
Monee, IL
15 July 2021